I0474441

Complete Guide To Blogging

(Everything you need to know to
turn you into a blogging unicorn)

By James Gaubert

PublishNation
www.publishnation.co.uk

Contents

2

1. The beginning of blogging

The word "blog" is a shortened form of "weblog".

In essence, a blog can be thought of as an online record of events, ideas, or other forms of expression, such as images and videos. Essentially it's a website that is usually structured using pieces of content, referred to as "posts".

How did blogging begin?

The word "weblog" was first used in 1997 to refer to regularly updated sections of websites in which the owner or owners would post media (usually text) describing events or opinions that had caught their interest.

The term "blog" was first used in 1999 by a programmer called Peter Merholz. In a short space of time, the concept of blogging and maintaining frequently updated websites centred on a particular topic became mainstream.

Moreover, other users could also comment on what they had written. Blogger.com was developed in 1999 and offered a similar service, allowing users a simple way to create their own blog, without the need for technical knowledge or an understanding of how to update web pages. WordPress and TypePad were then released in 2003.

Thanks to the introduction of these easy to use platforms, the number of blogs online increased by a huge amount between the late 1990s and the mid-2000s. It is estimated that by the mid-2000s, there were over 50 million blogs. Writers and freelance journalists began to realise that by blogging, they could potentially reach a large audience and share their opinions freely with other internet users.

Unlike the constraints imposed upon them in traditional printed form, they were not limited by word count, when it came to blog posts. Some of the most popular blogs of all time have been political in nature and even now still facilitate discussions on current affairs. At the time of writing, most reputable news sources, organisations and many prominent individuals maintain one or more blogs. They are seen as a useful means of spreading information and connecting people who share similar outlooks.

What kind of content do people share on blogs?

Most bloggers believe that an effective means of encouraging reader engagement and repeat visits is to use multiple types of media on their blogs.

In the early days of blogging, text was the main means by which bloggers could communicate their ideas. Since then, it has become increasingly common to see bloggers sharing their photos and videos with readers. A blogger may relate personal stories, share opinions, highlight links to other websites of interest and offer readers the chance to join an email list in order to keep themselves abreast of new posts and other developments on the blog. Bloggers may also make some documents and pieces of software available for downloading, either on a paid or free basis.

What about microblogging?

Traditional blogs take the form of webpages or websites that are updated frequently with content as deemed appropriate by the owner(s). However, another type of blogging came into existence in 2007. The most well-known type of microblogging platform is probably Tumblr.com, which allows users to sign up in order to create their own "Tumblr".

A Tumblr is a stream of content, sequenced in order of posting, uploaded or shared by the Tumblr's creator. Much like Twitter, it can be thought of as a combination of a blogging facility and a social network – users can easily post updates to their account and at the same time, engage with other members, sharing content and commenting on the online activity of other people. Twitter is usually classified as a social networking site rather than a means of creating a blog, as it limits its users' "posts" to just 280 characters. However, some users use it much like a diary and provide regular updates informing their followers of their everyday experiences.

2. Why do people write blogs?

There are a number of reasons why an individual might decide to start a blog, and its not always about making money! Some of the most common are as follows:

To find others who share their interests

This may be the most common motive for bloggers. When you create a blog that focuses on a particular topic or hobby, it will attract the attention of others who want or need to read about the same topic. This can result in online and offline friendships between those who enjoy talking about common interests, almost like modern day penpals. Most bloggers allow readers to comment on their posts and on blogs with high levels of traffic (i.e. a large readership), the discussions can be as well received and as eagerly anticipated as the posts themselves.

To help other people

Some bloggers are motivated to begin writing following an especially difficult or traumatic period in their own lives.

Others may be particularly passionate about an obscure hobby and wish to pass on instructions, hints, or tips via blog posts. Some bloggers may wish to explain their own unique worldview to readers, in the hope that it will help them make personal progress.

To record their journey at a turning point in their lives

Since the beginning of recorded history, people have used diary writing or journaling as a means of making sense of difficult times in their personal lives. This human tendency has not changed with the advent of the digital era. A blogger may choose to record their experiences as a mature student, a first time parent, the founder of a new business, or someone embarking on a mission to lose a significant amount of weight. They may want to record their progress as a means of motivating themselves, to inspire others, or to find other people who are undertaking similar challenges.

To create the kind of content they wanted to find online

Someone who has tried and failed to find exactly what they wanted to read online, whether that be articles about a niche interest or a website about a particular political ideology, may feel that they have no choice but to create it themselves.

As a means of creative expression

Now that bloggers can use images and videos alongside text to communicate their message, blogging has become more creative than ever before. Posts that are shared many times across the internet are referred to as having "gone viral", which is a sign of success in the blogging community. People with the ability to generate memorable content which conveys a memorable, important, or highly entertaining message, can soon accumulate readers, fans and followers. Some bloggers find the challenge of keeping the attention of an audience to be a positive stimulus to their creativity and enjoy thinking of new ways to keep them engaged.

Blogging usually entails writing and therefore can help the blogger improve their skills as an author. This can be helpful in improving their performance at work or school. This can apply to both fiction and non-fiction writers. Some fiction authors maintain blogs that not only allow them to connect with their readers and with other writers, but also allow them the chance to experiment with other types of writing, such as personal essays or literary criticism.

Artists, designers and photographers may also maintain blogs in which they showcase their latest designs or other creative work. This allows them to share ideas with others, to show their skills to potential employers or clients and to establish their identity as an artist.

As a form of activism

Blogging has become a powerful way for individuals who feel passionately about a cause or idea to spread their beliefs and attempt to change existing attitudes found within society. For example, the Tumblr blog stophatingyourbody.tumblr.com has received widespread attention and acclaim for its attempts to encourage readers to improve their self-esteem and question dominant narratives about beauty and attractiveness often found in the mainstream media. Online activism is often perceived as more democratic than traditional in-person action, as it allows anyone with an internet connection to get involved, regardless of their location, socio-economic status or other potentially limiting factors.

To establish themselves as a credible source or an expert in their field

By providing useful content on a regular basis, especially if it pertains to a particular subject, a blogger can establish themselves as an expert on their chosen subject. The internet as a whole is not moderated and it is theoretically possible for anyone to call themselves an "expert" and write as though they are in possession of vast amounts of knowledge on a certain topic, even if in reality they are no better informed than anybody else. However, it has also provided well qualified individuals with a platform that they can use to share valuable information. Experts with popular blogs can easily bolster their reputations as highly credible sources and they can then use their positive reputations as a means of attracting new business and networking opportunities.

As a therapeutic tool

Blogging can be commercial and large scale, as is the case for blogs found on major news websites. However, millions of blogs are written by individuals who share their innermost thoughts and feelings with the world as a healing process.

To fulfil coursework or academic requirements

As the internet in general and online journalism, in particular become more integral to our everyday lives, many colleges and universities offer courses in which blogging or creating an online presence is a mandatory part of the curriculum. For example, students studying journalism may have to publish regular public blog posts as part of their coursework. This ensures that they are equipped to deal with the demands of modern reporting and reader engagement, which involves digital publishing.

To feel a sense of achievement

Learning how to set up a blog, thinking of a suitable topic and maintaining a posting schedule can instil a sense of pride and achievement. Although blogging platforms are straightforward, setting up a blog entails picking up a new skill. This can feel like a big achievement for those who consider themselves poorly equipped when it comes to technical matters.

To promote their business or products

The use of online content to promote a product or a business is known as "content marketing". Running a blog, usually as part of a larger website, can provide potential customers with a reason to return to a company's website. This is a desirable outcome from the organisation's point of view, because it means that the reader will engage with the brand and therefore be more likely to consider spending money on products and services. Providing authoritative information, help sheets and tutorials free of charge instils a sense of goodwill in readers and is likely to improve their perception of the brand.

With the rise of social media, blogging is currently perceived as just one aspect of an organisation's or an individual's online presence.

It is common practice for a blogger to publish posts on their blog and then promote their content via various social media channels, in order to maximise its reach. Sometimes, a writer or artist will create a blog with the sole intention of promoting a certain product, concept, or exhibition.

As you can see, there are a great many reasons why someone would wish to start a blog. Anyone with an internet connection and an idea for a blog can try it out – and they can do so for free. For this reason, blogging is arguably one of the most democratic aspects of the internet. Everyone has the chance to write about whatever they wish – their lives and opinions. Blogging is not restricted to any age group, gender, socioeconomic class, or ethnic background. Moreover, anyone can blog in anonymity, which erases traditional divides still further.

3. Questions you should ask yourself before you begin blogging

Even if you intend for your blog to be just a hobby, it is still worth asking yourself why you wish to begin a blog in the first place and what you hope to achieve by setting up an online presence for yourself.

Here are a few questions you may wish to answer, before starting your blog, these questions can encourage you to consider your motives and to realistically gauge how much time and effort will be required to set up a blog.

What is the core message I want to communicate via my blog?

Most blogs fail when their owner lacks a sense of purpose and direction. Before you sign up for any blogging services or draft your first post, think about what you are trying to say. What is your reason for setting up a blog in the first place? If you had to summarise your blog's message in one sentence, what would it be?

Who am I targeting?

Once you are clear on the central message of your blog, you will be better placed to pinpoint who you are trying to attract. If you try to appeal to everyone, you will be disappointed. It's better to identify a target audience and then concentrate on serving their needs. Who is your ideal reader? What sex are they, how old are they, what are their primary concerns and what kind of lifestyle do they lead? If you would like to grow a significant readership over time, another consideration is how readily you will be able to target the audience you have in mind. Do you already have a following on social media and take part in online communities that cater to this demographic?

Do I have an idea of the content I will post to my blog?

This may seem an extremely obvious question, but it is essential for clarifying your blogging vision. What sort of experience do you wish to offer your readers and how will the content you provide help you to achieve that aim? Do you intend to write short essays, illustrate your points with images, curate content from other sources, provide step by step instructions, or structure your content in another way altogether?

What kind of media do I want to use on my blog?

Are you planning on using text-based media for the majority of your blog, or are you thinking of using images and videos? Think about your target audience, when making this decision. What kind of media will they respond to best? For example, if your blog is targeting young professionals, they may be less inclined to read long pieces of text, compared with a retired audience who may have more time in which to browse through lengthy essays. If you are trying to appeal to a young audience in their teens, videos and other visual media may be the best way of holding their attention. Look at other blogs targeted to your ideal audience. Learn from the way in which they present their content.

How much time will I need to set aside to set up and maintain my blog?

The answer to this question depends on several factors. Do you consider yourself to be comfortable with the internet and competent with computers in general, or will you require some time to become used to the online environment in which your blog will be situated? Do you feel confident in working with editing software? Do you have an understanding of how websites are hosted, or will you need to take time to understand terminology that may be new to you? Once you have got your blog up and running, you will need to schedule some time to create, edit and post new content. If you allow other people to comment on your posts, you will also need to factor in time for moderating and responding to their feedback. Ask yourself what, if anything, you will need to give up in order to keep your blog running. You may have to cut down on other online activities, such as gaming, or accept that your usual standard of housework may have to be lowered from time to time.

What resources or help will I need, in order to set up my blog?

Aside from this awesome book, will you need any further assistance or resources as you set up your blog? Perhaps you might feel more confident if you asked for and received help from a friend or relative who is already experienced in blogging or interacting with others as part of an online community.

Is there any reasonable chance that other people would be willing to contribute content to my blog?

It is common to feel a high level of enthusiasm and excitement when starting a new blog. However, the reality is that over time your motivation will begin to wane. Some days you may not want to create new content, even if you have promised yourself or your audience to update your blog. At times like this, it can be helpful to have a few eager contributors or guest bloggers to create posts for you. It's a good idea to think about who may be interested in contributing a guest post, at the beginning of your blogging journey.

Do I want to blog in such a way that reveals my identity?

The internet can be an unforgiving place and for this reason, it is not always a good idea to blog under your real name. In an ideal world, no one should have to fear online attacks or harassment (sometimes known as "cyber bullying" or "trolling"), but given the prevalence of online bullying, it is sensible to think carefully before starting a blog under your real name. There have been instances of online bullying against bloggers, which have later translated into in-person harassment and even violence. Most bloggers never encounter serious trouble online, but it is important to be aware that voicing your personal opinions online is not without risk.

The content of your blog and the context in which it is written are key factors to bear in mind, when deciding whether to use a pseudonym. If you are representing a business or writing on a non-controversial topic, it is likely that using your name and likeness is safer than if you are planning to write about more divisive issues. Some writers maintain two identities online – one as their "real self", which is appropriate for business related matters and contributions to non-controversial websites and another online identity which allows them to write about contentious issues, without fear of being targeted by those holding opposing views.

Am I comfortable with the fact that anything published on the internet may be permanently available to the general public for all time?

In theory, it is possible to take down a webpage or delete a blogpost, so that no one can ever read it again. However, in practice, the modern cliché "the internet is forever" is based on truth. Once you have posted something to the internet, anyone can take a screenshot of your work, share it with other people and copy your writing and images for future reference. Furthermore, there are websites such as Wayback Machine (archive.org) that hold archived copies of webpages, so that they are accessible to web users even if they have been deleted.

What does this mean for you as a blogger? Quite simply, you need to think carefully before publishing your thoughts, personal details, or likeness to a website. If you are planning to write under your real name, consider what kind of impression your blog will give to current and future employers, colleagues, partners and friends. This question is not intended to deter you from starting a blog, but you need to be aware that blogging is very much a public activity, which can result in personal difficulties or embarrassment if it is done without careful planning and concern for your reputation.

4. How to actually set up a blog

To run a blog, you will require a means of creating and managing your content (sometimes referred to as a Content Management System, CMS, or blogging software). Popular options include WordPress.

A host – This term refers to the website or service that will store and display your content as a blog on the internet. Free hosting is available on platforms such as Tumblr and Blogger and paid hosting is available from a number of companies, such as Dreamhost and Hostgator.

If you decide to self-host your blog, you will also need to purchase a domain name. This means that your blog's address will be yourblogname.co.uk, .com or any other available ending you choose to buy. You can also buy a domain name from a hosting provider such as those mentioned above and then link your domain with a blog that is hosted by another service.

Using a popular blogging platform versus starting a self-hosted blog

It is possible to set up a blog at no cost whatsoever.

However, setting up a free blog (or even upgrading to a paid account with more features) in this way comes with several drawbacks. These are as follows:

You will not have complete control over your blog's web address

If you use a blogging service such as Tumblr or Blogger, your blog address will take the form of yourblogname.thefreeservicename.com, or yourblogname.thefreeservicename.co.uk, rather than simply yourblogname.com, or yourblogname.co.uk. This is an important consideration, because your audience will have more respect for your blog if it has its own domain name.

Almost every well-respected blog has its own custom domain name. This means that you will either have to choose a blogging service that allows you to connect a domain name that you have purchased elsewhere or upgrade your free account with a blogging service that allows you the opportunity to buy a domain name as part of the deal. The alternative is to avoid using blogging websites and self-host your blog instead, by buying web hosting and a domain name before uploading your blog, using blogging software such as WordPress.

You and your readers may see advertisements when they view your blog

Companies providing free blog hosting have to cover their costs and one way in which they do this is via advertising. This means that if you sign up for a free blog, the service provider may use your blog as an advertising platform, which allows them to make money. This will make your blog appear less professional to those who view it. The solution is either to host your blog yourself, or to upgrade your hosting plan so that the advertisements are removed.

Most blogging platforms retain control over your content

When you post to a blog that a blogging service agrees to host for you (either for free or as part of a paid plan), you have far fewer rights and much less control over the content than if you choose to host it yourself. For example, Blogger and Tumblr can exercise the right to delete your blog and all of its content at any time, especially if someone complains that your content violates their terms of service. If you go down the self-hosted route, however, you can keep control over what is posted to your blog. This gives you a much greater degree of creative freedom.

Platforms that host free blogs may not allow you to monetize your work

When you pay for your hosting and domain name, you have much greater control over what advertisements (if any) you wish to accept onto your blog. Free hosting services may not allow you to take part in programmes that allow you to make money by hosting advertisements on your blog.

It is possible to transfer your content from a blogging service to a self-hosted setup at a later date, but this is not always simple

Some bloggers start their blogging careers by setting up an account with a popular blogging service and then move their blog content to a self-hosted site at a later date. In theory, this is a good idea, but in practice, it can be difficult to transfer all of your content and blog design to a new service.

5. Popular web options for building blogs

There are now so many free and paid blogging options available that a comprehensive overview of all would be a book within itself.

However, the following six platforms are widely used by the blogging community. A brief description of each, together with their pros and cons, is provided below

Blogger (blogger.com)

Cost: Free, with the option to add a domain name for around £10 per year

Blogger is one of the oldest and best-known platforms.

It is now owned by Google, meaning that if you have a Google account, you can use it to register for a Blogger blog. It is a free blogging option – Blogger lets you create content easily and will host it online for no charge. With this service, your blog address would be yourblogname.blogspot.com. If you buy a domain name from another provider, then you can use it with this service, but this may not be easy to do for beginners. Blogger is very simple to use, but also limited and basic in terms of design options. This means that you will not be able to customise your blog to the extent possible with some of the other services reviewed in this module. However, it may be a viable option if you are tentatively looking to explore the world of blogging and wish to keep everything fairly simple. There is no option to upgrade to a paid plan with extra features.

Medium (medium.com)

Cost: Free

Medium is a relatively young service, which allows you to open an account and start posting quickly and easily. It allows you to write and publish content for free. It is geared towards creatives, such as writers and artists and currently has over one million members. Your blog address would be medium.com/@yourblogname. As with Blogger, it is possible to use your own custom domain. The aesthetic is minimal – there is no way to customise your blog, meaning that although every blog owner can use text and images in any way they please within their posts, the overall look of each blog hosted by this site will be broadly the same. The interface is considered very simple to use, with the text editor having been designed to operate on a "what you see is what you get" basis.

Squarespace (squarespace.com)

Cost: After a free trial, prices start at £9 per month for a 20 page website

Squarespace is marketed as an all in one website solution for businesses, creatives and entrepreneurs. The service takes pride in the number of modern customisable designs it offers its users, although the sheer number available may be daunting for a beginner. It is also useful for those who want to run a blog with other people – the cheapest plan allows two people to log in and contribute to a blog separately, whereas the next upgrade (at approximately £14 per month) allows an unlimited number of writers to post blog content. This makes Squarespace a good choice for ambitious bloggers, who may want to create a magazine style blog sometime in the future. It also allows users to set up an online store, so if you plan to use your blog as a means of selling products or services, then Squarespace may be a good option for you.

Tumblr (tumblr.com)

Cost: Free, with the option of paying for customised themes that change your how your blog looks (costs vary)

Tumblr is both a blogging platform and a social media network. It is designed for bloggers who want to publish short pieces of content, such as short series of images, quotes and videos. When you sign up for free, you are assigned a blog address in this format: yourblogname.tumblr.com. It is possible to link your Tumblr blog to a domain name that you have purchased elsewhere. You can choose from many different designs, which means your blog can be customised, but the majority of designs are paid options that cost anywhere from approximately £5 to £40. Tumblr is considered one of the simplest blogging options available and many users enjoy the fact that there is a strong sense of community among Tumblr bloggers.

WordPress (wordpress.com/wordpress.org)

Cost: Free to set up a basic WordPress blog on wordpress.com.

You have the option to upgrade to paid plans that range in price from £2.50-£20.83 per month, which include custom domain names. You can also pay for customised blog themes, which vary in price. WordPress software (the program used to create blog content) is free to download from wordpress.org.

"WordPress" refers to both to a piece of software designed to produce blogs and the name of a blogging platform that will host your website on either a free or paid basis.

If you sign up to wordpress.com, you can build a blog using WordPress software. Your blog's default URL would be yourblog.wordpress.com. There are free and paid options for hosting your blog. The paid plans permit you to make more design changes to your blog, offering it a more customised feel. If you upgrade to a paid plan, you can also have advertisements removed from your blog, enjoy better customer support and have more storage space.

You can also add your own domain name via WordPress for around £15 per year, without upgrading to a paid plan, either when you sign up or later on in your blogging journey. If you elect to use any of the paid plans, a domain name is included. As WordPress is such a popular option, there is a strong sense of community and many tutorials available to help with common problems you may experience when building and maintaining a website.

However, the downside of using wordpress.com for building and hosting your website is that even if you use your own domain name and pay for increased customisation and storage space, WordPress still maintains ultimate control over your website and can take it down without warning if they believe your content to be objectionable.

In order to maintain total control over your blog and its content, you can instead pay for web hosting with a hosting provider that offers one-click WordPress software installation. This allows you to enjoy the capacities of this blogging system, without the restrictions you are subjected to when you sign up for hosting with wordpress.com. However, the downside is that this process is more complicated than signing up for a hosted blog at wordpress.com.

Ultimately, you need to make a decision as to how important it is that you retain control over your content and how much time and effort you can afford to spend on learning how to use new software. The WordPress community have developed a number of add-ons or "plugins" that can be downloaded and used to enhance your blog's functionality.

Wix (wix.com) – This is what I use for my blog, its so simple its almost idiot proof!

Cost: Free to set up a basic blog, then a range of premium plans are available from £5.16-£15.57 per month

Wix prides itself on offering anyone the chance to build an attractive website, with no technical background required. It offers a range of free and paid plans that vary with regards to how much content you can store on your website, whether your blog will contain advertisements and whether you have access to additional features such as the ability to build an online store and use forms on your website. It allows even those users with free plans the opportunity to customise their websites and their website builder is an easy to use drag and drop interface. However, although it is certainly possible to create a high quality blog using this platform, Wix was not designed specifically for bloggers.

Overall, it is simple to use, but it is not built with the assumption that the user will be posting content on a regular basis. To run a blog on the Wix platform, you will need to make use of the Blog Module within the Wix site builder. This is not complicated, but it may mean that setting up your blog takes a little longer than would be the case if you used the other options outlined above.

6. Choosing a suitable domain name for your blog

When you sign up to a hosting service, you will typically be asked whether you wish to buy one or more domain names for your website.

At this point, you will need to decide on an appropriate domain name for your blog. Here are a few factors to bear in mind:

The domain extension

You may be surprised at the range of extensions now available to those looking to buy a domain name. Along with .com, .co.uk and .net, there are now a multitude of more exotic extensions, such as .xyz, .photography and .pizza. Whilst these may look fun, a .com or .co.uk extension is more memorable and looks more professional. Unless you are certain that your blog will just be used as a creative outlet or as a hobby, choose a .com or .co.uk domain.

Length

Try to choose a relatively short domain name. This will make your blog's address more memorable and make it less likely that people will misspell the URL.

Memorability

Do not use hyphens, made up words or any other characters that make your domain name difficult to remember. Keep it concise. Acronyms, nicknames, jargon and foreign words are also best avoided.

Relevance

Your domain name should be relevant to the content of your blog. This will help potential readers remember your blog's name and it will also help to attract readers who first see your blog when they run a search for a related topic on Google. You should also think ahead if possible and consider whether your choice of domain name allows you to expand the number of topics you write about.

Do not be surprised if your first, second or even third choice of domain name is unavailable. With the sheer number of websites created every day, you may have to apply some creativity in coming up with alternative domain names. When you sign up for web hosting and attempt to register a domain, most hosting providers will provide you with alternative suggestions if your initial choice is already in use.

7. Where and how to get extra help in setting up your blog

For those new to blogging, especially those who do not consider themselves to be particularly competent with the internet or computers, the process of launching a blog can be difficult.

Fortunately, there are a number of options available to you, if you need further detailed guidance

If you are using a blogging platform, look for "help pages"

Each of the blogging websites listed in this chapter contain step by step guidance on how to set up a blog.

Don't be afraid to take advantage of this service – these companies will be well used to answering questions from beginners.

Look for step by step tutorials on YouTube

Go to the YouTube homepage (youtube.com) and search "blogging platform/service name" + "tutorial". This will bring up a list of videos that other users have put together, with the intention of helping those new to these sites. Try to use tutorials that have been posted within the past few weeks or months, as these are likely to be up to date. You can also locate tutorials by typing the same search terms into Google.

If you are self-hosting your blog, search for tutorials using the terms "set up self-hosted WordPress blog" + "web hosting provider's name". This will yield several video walk-throughs, which show you how to start a WordPress based website that works with your hosting provider.

If you are working with WordPress, invest in a good book that covers the technical side of running a blog

There are a number of good books available that take you through all the basic and more advanced functions of WordPress.

Consider hiring a freelance professional, if the process feels overwhelming

If you find the process of setting up a blog to be frustrating and you feel as though you are not making any progress, consider hiring someone to work with you. Look in your local Yellow Pages for a website designer. Call them and explain that you would like to set up a blog, but are not sure how or where to begin. You can also hire a freelancer via popular work for hire platforms, such as Upwork (upwork.com), Freelancer (freelancer.com) and People Per Hour (peopleperhour.com). Whether you work with a designer or another freelancer, it is a good idea to get several quotes before deciding who will get the job, because prices can vary widely. If possible, ask a friend or relative who is more confident with the internet in general to oversee the process, in order to make sure that the person you are hiring does not take advantage of you.

Ask a more knowledgeable friend or relative for help

If you know someone who already has a blog or a website, ask them whether they would mind showing you how to set up a blog of your own. They may be pleased to pass on their experience to you. It is easier to learn via "showing" rather than "telling", so consider asking them whether you could watch them add a new post to their blog and ask them to change various aspects, such as the colour scheme or background image, so that you can see how their blogging platform of choice works.

8. Choosing the right blog topic

You can invest a significant amount of time, effort and money into your blog and yet still fail to attract and hold the attention of potential readers, if you choose a topic that is of little interest to more than a handful of people.

If you only wish to blog for yourself and your immediate social circle, then it doesn't matter what you choose to write about. However, if you want to connect with others online, or even become a popular blogger in your area of interest, then you will need to spend several hours thinking through your options before even drafting your first blog post. This module assumes that you are starting a blog with the hope of attracting at least a modest following, including a group of regular readers who look to your writing as a source of valuable content. It will guide you through the process of selecting a blog topic, asking you to consider a number of questions that will help you narrow down your options. You will learn how to research the level of interest in your chosen topic and how to select a potentially profitable blog niche

How to generate an initial list of ideas for blog topics

What are my interests?

When you have free time, what do you enjoy doing? When you are with your friends, what do you most like to talk about? If you are reading a newspaper or magazine, what sections do you turn to first? When you are browsing in a bookshop, what kinds of titles tend to catch your eye?

If there is a particular topic that you could talk about for hours at a time, it could be a potentially strong topic for your blog. If you have no particular interest in a subject, you will find it hard to find the motivation to continue writing about it over the long haul.

Do not try and convince yourself that you will be able to make yourself care about a topic. Be honest with yourself – unless a subject area holds a real interest for you, do not make it the central focus of your blog.

What political or social causes do I care about most?

Are there any issues that keep you awake at night? When you are talking about current affairs with other people, are there any "hot button" issues that are almost guaranteed to elicit a strong reaction from you? Have you undergone any difficult personal experiences that have left you passionate about certain causes? If so, you may wish to consider writing a blog that keeps readers up to date with these issues.

If you are especially interested in politics or current affairs, you may wish to write a blog that tracks political developments in your country or in another part of the world. You could write from a particular political perspective or create a resource that takes various viewpoints into consideration. The latter idea could work well, if you are willing to collaborate with other writers whose opinions may differ to your own.

What am I best at?

When you consider the sheer scope of the self-help industry, it becomes apparent that there is a huge demand for useful information that can help people make better decisions in their personal lives. If you have been through a period of intense personal growth and are secure in your communication and relationship skills, this could be a fruitful source of blog material.

Am I looking to make money with my blog?

When you are deciding on a topic for your blog, think whether you are looking to build a fan base, make money, or both. It is important to realise that just because a blog is popular does not mean it is necessarily profitable – and vice versa. We will look in greater depth at the various options by which you can make money from your website. In the meantime, the basic principles to bear in mind if you are hoping to make money from a blog are as follows: Choose something with evergreen appeal (see the section below), choose something that appeals to a target audience who are willing and able to spend money on related products, choose a topic that interests you to a sufficient extent that you are willing to write about it for least one year and choose a blog topic that has the potential to help your readers solve a problem that is currently holding them back from living their ideal lifestyle.

Am I looking to acquire any new skills over the coming months and years?

If you are planning a change of career or are looking to develop your skillset in the near future, a blog may be the perfect means of tracking your progress. You could use a blog to pass on your new knowledge to other people, making mutually beneficial connections with others who are also looking to teach themselves how to do something new or build their knowledge in a particular area. This kind of blog can also be useful even when you have stopped publishing new posts, as it can serve as a repository of knowledge that others can learn from at a later date.

Allowing your audience to follow your progress – including any setbacks – will also help them to relate to you as an individual, which will broaden your appeal and encourage your readers to reach out and develop a relationship with you. If you wish to grow a popular blog, look to build a strong rapport with your audience. You can do this by responding to their comments and by taking on board their suggestions for future content.

Do I want to encourage the growth of a community via my blog?

The blogs with the strongest communities are frequently updated and feature posts on exciting or controversial content that has a strong personal meaning for the target audience.

If the idea of building an active, vocal following appeals to you, then it's important to make sure that your topic lends itself to plenty of posts that will appeal to your audience's imagination. Before you commit yourself to your chosen topic, spend a couple of hours mapping out potential post titles for your blog. If you cannot devise at least fifty, this is a sign that you need to choose a different topic or broaden the scope of your existing topic.

The power of research

Once you have identified a potential topic, get online and gauge the level of interest in those who may one day be your audience.

Fortunately, it has never been easier to use the internet to establish what people wish to read about, what they are willing to spend money on and which of their personal problems they are most willing to solve. Here are a few ways in which you can use online research, to gauge the popularity of your topic:

Run a series of basic Google searches

Write down a list of keywords related to your proposed blog topic and then run them through Google.

Do your searches return a lot of results, featuring pages that have been updated fairly recently? This is a good sign, as it suggests a lot of people are writing about the topic.

Look at the topics addressed by large lifestyle sites and blogs

Well known lifestyle websites such as Lifehacker (lifehacker.org) and the Huffington Post (huffingtonpost.com) are good barometers of public interest and opinion. Skim the main headings of each section. Which articles receive the most comments and feedback?

Remember that large websites have the resources required to research the latest and upcoming trends – take full advantage of this fact.

If certain issues come up on a frequent basis, they may make a good topic for your blog. At the same time, be aware that trends change by definition. A good approach is to combine a trending topic with evergreen content and concerns (see below for more on the concept of evergreen blogs).

Find out what affiliate marketers are selling that relates to your topic of choice

Researching what is selling well online can give you a valuable insight into your audience's concerns and desires – useful knowledge when it comes to writing content that makes an appreciable difference to peoples' lives and thereby growing your reputation in the process. A simple way of gauging the strength of a market is to look at the extent to which those trying to sell to the target demographic are succeeding. To make the most of the information available freely online, you need to have an understanding of affiliate marketing and how it relates to blogging and other online content.

In brief, affiliate marketing is the practice of promoting another person's product or service in exchange for a commission on every sale.

Warning signs that you have chosen the wrong topic for your blog

Here are some indications to watch out for:

There are few books for sale on your topic

It is a mistake to try and devise a completely original blog idea. Instead, a better strategy is to write about topics that have been proven to "work" and already attract a following on existing blogs and other platforms. Do not be afraid to enter a niche that is already well populated by bloggers and other online personalities. A quick test that will tell you in minutes whether people are interested in your topic is to go to Amazon or another online book retailer and type in a few words relating to your topic. If there are many books available for sale and they each have multiple reviews, this is an encouraging sign that there is an audience out there who are willing and ready to read about your topic. If you can find well received books that point you to a blog in their description, then so much the better – this implies that the author has managed to set up a successful blog based around their topic and found an audience willing to pay money for related books (and possibly other paid resources as well).

You are trying to combine two topics that ought not to be combined

Some bloggers attempt to broaden their blog's appeal by catering to two audiences. Sometimes, this is an effective strategy, but too often it results in a blog that lacks focus.

You may be tempted to split your posts so that the first is targeted towards one group, the second post to the other group and so on. However, the outcome will be a patchwork blog that does not attract a stable target audience.

You cannot find any popular blogs on the topic

If you can locate at least five active blogs that have endured for several years and centre around your particular topic, this is a good sign that people have been looking for information on a particular topic and that they will continue to do so for years to come. Do not make the mistake of thinking that established bloggers have completely dominated your chosen niche – there is always room for writers who can approach a topic from a new angle or write with a distinctive new voice.

Remember too, that well-established bloggers may feel restricted in the content they can post or the extent to which they can change the direction of their blog, because they do not want to risk alienating their audience.

As a new blogger, this puts you at an advantage – you can take risks in presenting content in a new way, because you do not yet have to worry about upsetting those who have been following you from the very beginning.

You cannot find any well-liked Facebook pages on the topic

Facebook is still one of the most influential social networks and so is a good barometer of the internet's interest in particular topics. When you start narrowing down your list of potential blog topics, search for Facebook pages that pertain to your interest and look at how many "Likes" are associated with the first 10-20 results. In general, more than 10,000 "Likes" is a positive sign, but the more the better.

You cannot find any relevant Twitter accounts with more than 50,000 followers

Look for leaders and influencers who already write about your topic and sell related products and services. Ideally, you will be able to find several people who have at least 50,000 other Twitter users following them. If you cannot find any thought leaders in your niche, this is a sign that you will struggle to locate a target audience for your blog.

You cannot find any trade associations or organisations based around your topic or target audience

The easier it is to define your audience, the easier it will be to reach them. Think about who will be interested in, or benefit from, your posts. For example, if you are writing about the creative process that goes into writing fiction, your target audience may be described as "beginning fiction writers" or just "writers". Writers, like many other groups, have a strong sense of identity. Ideally, to maximise your blog's reach and popularity, you need to appeal to a group of people who take pride in holding a certain identity and are eager to apply a particular label to their "tribe".

Your topic does not fit into any of the "evergreen categories"

One of the key principles of marketing is that people all over the world are broadly alike in that they share similar concerns and challenges. These common difficulties are useful to writers, bloggers and marketers, because they present an opportunity to create "evergreen content". Evergreen content does not date or become irrelevant, because it addresses universal human concerns.

An overview of five evergreen categories is outlined below.

Health and fitness

Every year, millions of people attempt to get fit and lose weight. Weight loss is therefore an example of a huge niche that, when executed properly, can attract a reliable following. In our increasingly sedentary society, there is also an unprecedented interest in physical fitness, exercise and strength training. Within this broad category, there are numerous viable sub-niches, including diet plans aimed at mothers, exercise regimens aimed at busy professionals and exercise plans suitable for those with specific health problems. Common mental health problems such as anxiety and depression also attract a large audience.

Dating and relationships

Most people list relationships as one of their chief concerns in life. Blogs, books and courses that advise readers how to successfully start and grow a happy relationship are highly sought after. Relationship skills are important for both romantic and non-romantic relationships and so there is a never-ending demand for content that helps people sharpen their communication skills and resolve difficulties in relationships.

Finance

Many people wish that they could earn more money, or put the money they already have to better use. For this reason, blogs that give people practical tips on how to save money and build a more secure financial future are often popular. Debt management is another topic that attracts many readers who may be desperate to improve their financial status.

Education

The cost of going to college or university can be prohibitive for most people and so many are looking to the internet for free or low-cost alternatives. Blogs that teach valuable skills which may improve an individual's chances of promotion or even help them embark on a new career are likely to be well received. Another angle within the education niche is study skills and tips for students who want to achieve good grades, whilst expending the least amount of effort.

Self-improvement

Human nature is such that we often try and improve ourselves in order to secure more fulfilling work, higher status and greater mastery over our self-perceived weaknesses. As a result, there is a flourishing self-improvement (also known as the "self-help") industry dedicated to helping people become happier, more motivated and more successful in their personal and professional lives. This is a broad category, which includes topics such as confidence-boosting, goal-setting, increasing personal productivity and obtaining a sense of purpose in life. There is often an overlap with dating and relationship related content.

If your blog topic does not fit any of the above categories, you may find it hard to attract a sizeable audience.

It is certainly possible to develop a successful blog that is not based on an evergreen topic, but if you are serious in finding an audience and helping them solve problems, then it is sensible to ensure that you are blogging on a subject that resonates with many people

9. Content content content!!!

Even if you have chosen a popular blog topic and have an idea that will help you to present the topic in a new way that will make you stand out from your competitors, your blog will never be successful unless you learn how to publish posts that draw readers in and then encourage them to come back for more. In the following sections, we will look at practical ways in which you can generate meaningful content that will deliver your message to your audience.

You will have noticed that bloggers make use of a number of formats when they post. Some of the most common post formats are outlined below, along with the pros and cons of each. You will soon notice that the fit between a post's content and format is important

Regular articles

These are text-based posts, which are often based around factual matters. There is no absolute rule when it comes to the ideal length for an article, but a typical blog post ranges from around 500-1,500 words. They should have a clear beginning, middle and end – that is, the reader should understand within the first paragraph what will be addressed in the post, before being steered through a series of relevant points presented in a logical order. A good article will also feature a definitive conclusion that summarises the key issues raised within the piece, before posing a question or recommendation to the audience

Authority posts

These posts are usually significantly longer than regular articles. Bloggers publish authority posts with the intention of establishing themselves as thought leaders or experts in a particular niche.

Typically, they will be several thousand words in length and will aim to provide the reader with a complete outline regarding a specific topic or idea. They may be text-based, but many will make use of images and videos. They may include a tutorial or set of step by step instructions.

Authority posts are an excellent way to establish credibility and they are often widely shared within a community, if they are well written. This means that they have enormous potential to increase your visitor numbers and boost your reputation. However, they require a large initial investment in terms of time and effort, which may not be worthwhile if the post does not attract much attention.

Lists

If you wish to provide your audience with a set of facts, figures or arguments, then a list format may be a good choice for your blog post. Lists can be numbered or simply presented in bullet points. They may be text-based or incorporate other elements, such as photographs or illustrations. Lists can also be a good way of distilling a complicated idea down to its most basic components or transmitting the very basics of what the reader ought to know about a particular topic.

Lists are quicker and easier to read than paragraph-based articles and tend to be more readily shared by those who read them. They can also (but not always) be quicker to write than regular articles. However, lists do not carry quite as much gravity as other post formats, such as tutorials and authority posts

Videos

Sometimes video is a more effective format when trying to communicate a message, compared with text or images. You can either make your own videos in order to convey your message or use those created by others (with permission). Video offers you the chance to appear to your readers as a real, live human being. This can be put to good use, if you want to make an appeal or announcement on your blog, or if you just want to offer your readers some variety.

Video is often perceived to be a more immediately engaging format, compared to text or static images – and it can convey a lot of meaning in a relatively short amount of time. However, if your readers come to believe that you are relying on videos (especially if you do not make them yourself) rather than taking the time to write high-quality content, they may lose respect for you as a blogger and source of information.

Simplified explanations

Simplified explanation-style posts are a cross between an authority post and a tutorial. They typically take a complicated concept and break it down into basic steps. For example, a blogger who writes about global politics may choose to write a simple guide to understanding the historical source of current tensions in the Middle East. Simplified explanations are typically longer than typical text-based posts, but shorter than in-depth tutorials or authority posts.

Posting a good simplified explanation can help to establish you as a helpful source of knowledge on your topic.

Much like tutorials, simplified guides are often widely shared if they are well written. They are a valuable resource, for those new to a topic or who are just getting started in developing a particular skillset. However, more knowledgeable readers may feel patronised or bored, if they are presented with this kind of content on a regular basis.

Curated resources

A curated post consists of a list of links to other online articles, videos, or any other content that a blogger believes would be of interest to their audience. It is quite common for bloggers to present a weekly "round-up" post, whereby they take the opportunity to signpost their readers to external links that will entertain them or further their knowledge
Publishing this kind of post can build your credibility as someone who keeps themselves up to date with recent news and developments on your topic. Curated posts can also act as a useful tool for networking with other bloggers – if you tell someone that you have provided a link to their work on your website, they may well return the favour at a later date. However, if you use curated posts on a frequent basis, your readers may conclude that you are unwilling or unable to

produce original content. This may cause your reputation to suffer.

Inspirational/Conceptual posts

If you have devised what you believe to be a truly new idea concerning your niche or subject area and feel excited about it, you may wish to publish an inspirational or conceptual post in which you outline your vision or beliefs.

When they are well written and structured in a logical fashion, this kind of post can be exciting for readers who are willing to see the world around them in a new way. However, overly long conceptual posts can appear somewhat self-indulgent. They are best published on an occasional basis only.

10. Coming up with awesome ideas for your blog posts

Bloggers who post on a regular basis stand the best chance of establishing an audience.

However, the prospect of coming up with an ongoing stream of new ideas for blog content can feel overwhelming. The good news is that if you have chosen your blog topic carefully in accordance with the guidelines contained within previous modules, you need never worry that you will run out of ideas. You also have access to the internet and to other bloggers' websites – and these two resources alone will guarantee you a never-ending supply. Here are a few ways of generating more ideas for content, whenever you feel stuck

Find out what problems your target audience are facing

To connect with your target audience, you need to understand their concerns and write about them. Read the comments sections on other websites, look at posts on forums that serve your target audience and browse Facebook discussions on public groups. Make a list of the topics and queries that emerge on a regular basis and address them in future blog posts. What practical tips and help can you offer your audience? What kind of content will inspire them to overcome their difficulties?

Ask yourself what you most wanted to know when you began learning about your topic

Can you remember what it was like to be a beginner in your field, or how it felt when you were just starting to learn about your blog topic? What were your most urgent questions? Write a post or series of posts in which you address these issues.

Watch the news

Keep up to date with current affairs. When you browse the headlines or listen to news stories, think about the potential connections between your blog topic and what else is going on in the world around you. For example, if you are a knitting blogger who hears a news item about the link between creativity, hobbies and mental health, then this could provide you with inspiration for a post about the positive effects of knitting for those who need to de-stress.

Read or watch something you would never normally pay attention to

Sometimes you may find yourself stuck in a rut, unable to think of any new ideas whatsoever. A quick way to shake yourself free is to expose yourself to new ideas and media that you usually avoid.

Look at some inspiring images

If you primarily work with words, spend some time looking at images that uplift and inspire you. As well as improving your mood, which will in turn improve your ability to relax and think of new ideas, an image can inspire you in a literal sense. For example, if you view a series of images showing exotic holiday destinations, you may feel inspired to write about travel or vacations in a way that relates to the topic of your blog.

Find some inspirational quotes and use them as a basis for a post

Do you have a favourite quote that you return to whenever you need inspiration or encouragement? Create a post that explains why this quote has meaning for you and tie it back to the topic of your blog.

Decide on a post format and then on a topic

Instead of devising a topic and then choosing a format, try choosing a format – perhaps one you have not tried before – and then think of a message or content that would fit with your choice. For example, if you have never used a list on your blog before, set yourself the challenge of devising a ten-point post that gives your readers some unusual or fun facts relevant to your blog topic

Use services that show you what people have been searching for

Google, Twitter and Reddit can all provide you with valuable ideas for blog posts, by showing you what is currently trending online. Once you are equipped with this information, you can then use your creativity to draw links between a particular trend and the central topic of your blog.

Google allows the general public to see what their users want to find on the internet. You can use Google Trends (google.com/trends), to find out what people have been looking for online over the past 24 hours and in various different countries. Google currently operates in 100 countries. You can also browse trends by categories, including Health, Business and Sports. Twitter (twitter.com) features trending topics and discussion points on its homepage. Reddit – referred to as "the front page of the internet" – shows you the most popular stories and news items on its homepage (reddit.com).

Look at chapter headings in books about your topic

Go into a bookstore – whether online or on the high street – and pick up a few books on your topic. Look at the chapter titles and major subheadings. Could you use any of these as prompts for your next blog post?

You could also flip to the back of the book and look through the index for useful words and phrases that could form the basis of a blog post, or at least give you an idea for future avenues of research.

Read other blogs on your topic

This is one of the best ways of ascertaining what your audience wants to read about. Bookmark at least three successful blogs in your niche and read them on a regular basis. Take note of the issues they cover and then ask yourself how you could do it better. Remember that whilst it is not acceptable (or legal) to copy someone else's work, there is nothing wrong with taking inspiration from someone you admire.

Write about your successes and your failures

Even if the tone of your blog sways towards the formal, consider publicly reflecting on your personal successes and failures – at least as they relate to blogging. What has gone well on your blogging journey so far and what would you do differently next time? Personal posts allow your readers to gain an insight into your character and background as they learn from your blog.

Attend an event related to your blog topic and then write about it

If you can find a conference or festival that fits with the content of your blog, attend it and
write about your experiences.

Find out what products are popular with your audience and review them

If members of your target demographic have begun to show an interest in a particular product or service, why not write a blog post about it? If the product or service is inexpensive or comes with a free trial, you could review it yourself and write a post about your experience.

When you become a well-established blogger with a consistent audience, you may be able to secure free review copies of books, courses and other products, by getting in contact with the retailer and explaining that you are interested in reviewing their product for your blog.

Think about incorporating a new, regular feature on your blog

If you feel as though your blog is becoming a little stale and you need to vary the format of
your posts, consider experimenting with a new regular feature on your blog.

Ask someone else to write a guest post for your blog

Approach another blogger in your niche and ask them to contribute a post to your blog. This will provide your readers with a new perspective, as well as giving you a brief respite from creating content for your site. You could either provide them with several options for topics, or give them free reign.

11. The power of a posting calendar and schedule

It is possible to think of new blog post ideas and write them on a weekly or daily basis, as required. However, most people benefit from planning their posts well in advance. If you know that you have the material required to sustain your blog for the foreseeable future, this will alleviate any stress experienced by trying to think of new ideas on a regular basis. You don't need to draft every post in advance but try to include at least two or three brief sentences in the final column, which will give you a prompt when writing your post.

Allow yourself at least a few hours to complete your three-month posting schedule. It may take a while before your ideas start flowing, but if you have selected a suitable blog topic that holds your interest, then you should be able to complete a posting schedule that covers the coming months. Make sure you keep it up to date with new ideas and cross off posts as you complete and publish them. If you work best when you have a tangible reward to look forward to, write down each reward associated with each post or milestone.

How to add extra value to your blog posts

With a few simple adjustments, you can elevate a good blog post into a valuable piece of content that your audience will be eager to share with others.

The following tips are useful ways of improving the perceived quality of your work:

Quote authority figures

You should already be following the online activities of thought leaders in your field, so put your efforts to good use and cite them occasionally in your articles. This will show your readers that you are taking the time to keep up to date with important figures in your niche. Moreover, you can then contact the individual in question to let them know that you have quoted them in one of your articles. Successful bloggers are often keen to help others, because they know this improves their own reputation, so they may well draw attention to your work on their own blog or social media feed. We will return to the issue of working with other bloggers in a later module.

Back up your claims with scientific research

Most people are familiar with Google, but relatively few people make use of Google Scholar (scholar.google.com). A database containing millions of scientific journal articles, book extracts and other pieces of peer-reviewed content, Scholar can be an excellent resource when you want to back up a point you make in a blog post with some scientific research.

End your post by spelling out the implications of this information for your readers

Even if you believe the implications of your post are obvious, state them clearly at the end. Remind the reader that they have made a good decision in spending time reading your blog. Round your post off by asking your readers to leave their comments and feedback. If you have written a lengthy post, including a brief summary for the benefit of readers who may have read the post in two or more sittings and have forgotten the points you made near the beginning. Writing a summary will also benefit you, as you will quickly be able to pick up on any missing content and identify places where the content does not flow as smoothly as you would like.

Use correct spelling, punctuation and grammar

You do not have to be a gifted writer to build a popular blog. However, the more polished your writing, the more seriously you will be taken by your audience. If you are unsure whether you have spelled a word correctly, always double check before you publish a post. If possible, read over your posts at least three times before they go live. Your readers will not mind the occasional mistake, but they may lose patience if every post is littered with errors. You should also make sure that you make appropriate language choices. If you are not completely certain as to the meaning of a word or whether it is offensive, always take the time to double check before sending your writing out into the world. Bad language is best avoided, unless it is expected and appreciated by your target audience.

12. Making money from your blog

So this is the part everyone wants to know....how do you make money from your blog!

It is important to note that even in the best-case scenario, making a lot of money in a short space of time is not a reasonable goal. It is best to view blogging as a potential side business and means of making some extra income, rather than a full-time profession.

Making money via advertising

One of the most common ways of monetizing a blog – or any kind of website – is via advertising.

The basic idea is simple – you set aside some space on your blog for an advert and then join a network or scheme that connects you with people who wish to pay for advertising space online. There are three main types of adverts that bloggers can use to generate income – Cost Per Click (CPC) adverts, Cost Per Impression (CPI/CPM) adverts and private adverts.

Cost Per Click (CPC)/Pay Per Click (PPC) adverts

When you agree to host this kind of advertisement on your website, you are paid by the advertisement network, every time a visitor to your blog clicks on it. These adverts are usually presented as banners, which you can position on your blog pages.

When you use one of these programmes, you do not have to deal with the advertisers yourself. Instead, the adverts that get placed on your website will be chosen by the company you sign up with and they will also oversee your payments. These companies host ongoing online "auctions", in which advertisers compete to buy the chance to place their adverts on webpages (including blogs) that are relevant to their products or services.

When you join a network, you will be given exact instructions as to how you can post adverts to your blog. Typically, this involves copying and pasting a piece of code into the software you use, to create blog posts or make changes to your blog's appearance, but each company has their unique step by step guide. The amount of money you can make by hosting CPC or PPC adverts will depend on several factors and could be as little as a few pennies per click or up to several pounds, or more. If your blog is in a popular niche in which advertisers try and sell high-end products such as luxury items or expensive diet and exercise solutions, you can expect to earn more on average than if you are creating content centred on a less popular or profitable niche. Another vital factor is the quality and longevity of your website.

Advertisers will happily pay more to advertise on a well-established blog with long form content, compared with a new blog or one with only light content.

You also need to bear in mind if you are taking part in a CPC programme that your profits will depend in no small part upon your ability to attract people to your blog who will actually click on the adverts. In other words, you need to write content that consistently attracts people who are sufficiently hungry for information or a solution to their problems, that they will want to know more about the product or service promoted. If your content shows up in search engine results, you will enjoy better results if it hooks in readers keen for a solution.

Cost Per Impression (CPM, also known as "Cost Per 1000 Impressions") adverts

When you host a CPM advertisement, you are paid based on how many readers view the advert, rather than how many click it. For every 1,000 people who view the advert, you will receive a fixed amount of money. The amount of money paid per 1,000 impressions can vary from a few pence to over £10. CPM adverts can take the form of banners, buttons, popups and even videos. Two of the most popular CPM networks are AdsOptimal (adsoptimal.com) and PropellerAds (propellerads.com). There is little point in trying to make money with CPM advertisements, unless you have a steady stream of traffic to your site. Unless you have thousands of visitors per day, this avenue will not be profitable, even though some CPM will accept sites that do not yet have much traffic. It is best to think of CPM as a potential money-making avenue to explore once your site is established and you are seeing a reliable number of visitors on a daily basis.

Private adverts

You can also sell advertising space directly to interested parties. If your blog becomes successful, you may find that retailers get in contact with you and ask whether you would consider hosting an advert for their product on your blog. You can also research companies that seem to be a good fit with your blog's message and offer them the chance to promote their products and services on your website.

The advantage of selling advertising space in this way is that you can set your own rates and keep all of the money paid by the advertiser, neither of which are possible when working with the advertising networks described above.

However, you need to ensure that all parties understand the terms and conditions of the transaction, as you will not be able to fall back on a third party to mediate in the event of any disputes. Private adverts can take the form of banners, buttons, links within written content, or even sponsored posts in which you promote an advertiser's product. You may decide to charge a one-off fee to post a link or to publish a sponsored blog post, or you can offer the advertiser the opportunity of paying for a banner or button on a weekly or monthly basis. Typically, an advertiser will supply their own advertisements and branding for you to use.

Affiliate marketing

Affiliate marketing is another means of making money by promoting someone else's products and services on your blog, but it goes further than conventional advertising.
When you act as an affiliate, you promote a product or service on your blog in exchange for a commission on every sale secured via your site. If you choose products that tie in to your blog's niche, this can be an excellent means of making money, as long as you attract enough visitors. For example, if you run

a blog about weight loss, you could choose to promote a weight loss supplement. Every time a reader makes a payment, the vendor will pay you a commission.

Depending on the product and vendor, this could be up to 75% or more.
Bloggers who work as affiliates often use programmes such as Clickbank (clickbank.com) or JVZoo (jvzoo.com) to find a suitable product or products to promote. Just as with advertising, your success will depend both on the quality of the traffic you get to your blog and on the fit between your blog's content and the products and services you are looking to promote. Vendors looking for affiliates to promote their products will often be willing to supply promotional material, such as banner advertisements or even articles, which you can publish on your blog. You can also use affiliate links in your articles, giving your readers a quick and easy way to immediately purchase the product or service mentioned

Successful affiliate

The most successful affiliate marketers are those who have built a loyal following who perceive them to be authority figures within a particular niche. If you have a good looking website and a reputation as a trustworthy individual who knows a lot about your blog topic, your readers will listen when you recommend that they try a certain product. You can then refer them on to the vendor via a special link that they will provide and then you will be paid a pre-agreed amount of commission for every sale.

Setting up an email newsletter is a great way of building an audience of receptive individuals, whom you can sell to over and over again.

Remember, it is easier to keep selling to a loyal customer than to win new business. However, it is important to remember that most people do not like the feeling that they are being "sold to", so keep blatant sales pitches to a minimum.

In addition, you should only promote products and services that you truly believe in and ideally have used yourself. If you can provide your readers with an honest, comprehensive, yet positive review of a product, they will hold you in higher esteem than if you merely urge them to make a purchase. You should always make it clear, if you are writing a particular post with the intention of promoting someone else's product. Never promote irrelevant products to your audience, in the hope of making a quick profit. This strategy often backfires, when readers choose to spend their time on other blogs instead.

Selling your own products via your blog

Along with affiliate marketing, the most potentially profitable way of making money from your blog is to use it as a platform from which to sell your own products.

It has never been easier to sell books, eBooks, courses and other resources from a website. You do not need extensive technical knowledge to set up an online store. If you have a self-hosted WordPress blog, you can use a plug-in such as WooCommerce (woocommerce.com) or Easy Digital Downloads (easydigitaldownloads.com). If you are using a blogging service to host and run your site, such as Squarespace or Wix, you will probably have access to the tools you need to build an online store as part of your account package. These tools allow you to list and describe the products you have for sale, to handle transactions in a secure manner and to keep records of all purchases your customers have made.

The amount of money you make will obviously be dictated by the price of your products and the number of people willing to buy them. In theory, it is possible to make large profits if the products you are offering are of high quality and offer your target audience a clear solution to their problems. You may need to invest time and money in creating and improving your products, but the effort could pay off in the long term.

What kinds of products could you create to sell from your blog?

You can sell digital or physical products from your blog, but most bloggers who make money from their own products do so by selling digital products, such as eBooks, information packs and courses.

The advantage of creating and selling your own products is that you get to retain complete creative control over the process. You also get to keep all of the profits from each sale and can choose how you advertise each product (some affiliate marketing networks and vendors place restrictions on how you can advertise their products). In addition, you do not have to worry about a third party going out of business and cutting off your earning potential, as can happen when promoting products as an affiliate.

The importance of listening to feedback from your audience

Some bloggers make the mistake of pushing the needs of their audience to one side in their pursuit of profit.

This is a serious error, because without traffic, a blog will not generate a healthy income. If you start advertising on your blog, promoting other peoples' products or selling your own, make sure that you are not doing so at your readers' expense If you are selling your own products, take every review seriously. You cannot hope to please everyone, but if the same issues are raised in multiple reviews, then you should consider removing the product from sale and refining it in line with your customers' feedback. Consumers always like to feel as though their opinions have been taken into consideration and if you show that you are willing to put their needs as a priority, then they will be quicker to trust you in the future.

Selling services on your blog

Once you have established yourself as an authority within a particular niche, you may be able to sell your services along with, or instead of, your products.

Taking this step can be extremely lucrative, but it is vital that you understand your limitations and what you can and cannot promise your customers. Never state or imply that you are trained or qualified in a particular area, unless you have the relevant credentials to support your claims. Always make it clear to your clients that whilst you can advise them to follow a specific course of action, you are not responsible for the final outcome. It is sensible to consult a legal professional, who can help you draw up a contract that the client must sign before receiving your services. This way, you protect yourself from any potential legal trouble that may arise as a result of a client's unrealistic expectations.

You should also take care not to overbook or over-commit yourself early on in your consulting career. It is best to take on only a couple of clients at a time, when you are starting out. As you gain more experience, you will be better placed to understand how much time each client typically requires. You can then make a sensible estimate as to how many clients you can handle in any given time period.

Why blogging is not a get-rich-quick scheme

It is definitely possible to make money with a blog – and some bloggers have even been able to give up their regular job and use their blog as their sole source of income.

However, the majority of people who try to make money online will not be this successful. It takes patience and a great deal of hard work, to build a respected blog that attracts the visitor numbers required to make an ongoing profit. If you want to make money from advertising, you will need to devise a long-term content strategy that builds your blog from a basic website to a popular online authority.

Even if you publish excellent content on a regular basis and reach out to other bloggers (we will look at this in further detail in the next module), it will take time to grow a following. You may need to advertise your blog and your products on social media, a topic to which we will return later on in the course.

13. Networking with other bloggers to build reach

Why you are more likely to be successful when you work with others

The world of blogging can be daunting, when you are setting up your first blog and learning how your platform of choice works.

You may be concerned about blogging etiquette, the norms you need to learn and follow within your niche and how you can avoid the most common beginners' mistakes. Fortunately, there is one strategy you can use that will help you find answers to most of your questions and build your website's reputation into the bargain – networking with other bloggers. In this module, you will learn how to connect with other bloggers and in doing so, promote your work. We will look at how you can network both offline and in person and consider the benefits of attending conferences held especially for bloggers.

Here is an overview of why you should consider following others within your niche and making contact with them right from the inception of your blog:

You will be able to learn from the mistakes of others, rather than repeating them yourself

Many bloggers are keen to pass on their knowledge and experience to those new to the community (sometimes referred to as the "blogosphere"). If you have a question about blogging – whether it be related to trouble you are having with a plugin, or a question about how best to structure posts – don't be afraid to reach out to a blogger you admire with a short email, a comment on one of their posts, or a quick message on social media.

Note that this does not mean you should ask them to set aside a significant amount of time to help you with your problems or to promote your blog, merely that people are often flattered by simple questions that will only take them a moment or two to answer.
People feel good about themselves when they are given the opportunity to help others at little cost to themselves – and professional bloggers know that when they are seen to offer assistance to those in need, their reputation will receive a boost.

Take an hour or two to look through your fellow bloggers' oldest content and take note of how they have changed their blogging style over time.

If you decide to enable comments on your blog, you need to prepare yourself for the possibility of negative and even hostile feedback. You can learn much from others, when it comes to deciding on a strategy ahead of time for dealing with readers' negative opinions.

Some bloggers like to set out what they have learned about blogging in dedicated blog posts. If your favourite bloggers have been running their websites for a year or more and have been posting on a regular basis, search their site for any posts that outline their thoughts on running a blog. They may well have decided to list their mistakes and how they have used them as a springboard for progress, or they may have written several essays on how they apply general principles of blogging to their everyday writing practice.
Either way, you could pick up a number of useful tips from reading this kind of post.

Be an asset to the blogging community and build your reputation

Assuming you have the time, try your best to be an asset to the blogging community.

As your online presence grows and your blog acquires a reputation, new bloggers may approach you with questions similar to those you asked at the start of your blogging career. Offer as much help and advice as reasonably possible. Even if you receive no immediate reward, you can take pride in knowing that you have tried to assist someone else.

You will gain valuable insight into the issues of most concern to your target audience

If your primary concern is growing a loyal following, you will want to gain an insight into the wants, needs and problems that preoccupy your target audience. There are few more effective ways of gaining this knowledge than by paying close attention to what other people in your field are writing about. You should also read feedback left by their readers and note any themes that come up on a recurring basis. These topics could form the basis for a popular blogpost, or even a series.

You should also look at the products or services being offered for sale. This will give you a valuable insight into how much disposable income your target audience has to spend, as well as the things they are willing to spend it on. If possible, read the reviews they are leaving on other bloggers' products. This will give you valuable information, if and when you decide to sell your own products and services later on.

You will be able to spread the word about your blog and amplify your message

When you communicate with another blogger, whether it be on their website or via social media, you will often have the opportunity to post a link back to your site or your most recent post. As long as your content is of good quality and relates to their work, a blogger in your niche may well draw their readers' attention to your site in their posts. The most successful bloggers do not waste time worrying about the competition reading other blogs, because they are secure in their ability to produce useful content that will keep their audience returning over the long term.

If you contribute comments to a "big name" blog on a regular basis, you will become a known name within that community and so other blog readers will feel a sense of curiosity that drives them to look at your own site. Don't forget to continue making constructive contributions once your blog becomes popular.

If you and another blogger possess diverse skills, you can trade services, help each other out!

It is possible to create a blog based solely around text, but this type of blog is becoming increasingly rare, as bloggers make use of other media, such as images and videos, to capture their readers' attention. This allows for greater creative expression, but also means that bloggers need to develop an increasing number of different skills, or at least understand how to outsource particular tasks. However, if you network with other bloggers who have a skillset different to your own, you may well be able to trade tasks so that both of you can save time and money.

You may make new friends, or make contact with potential business partners, it's all about networking!

When you network with other bloggers, you have the opportunity to meet people who have set themselves similar goals to you. You can therefore encourage one another when your motivation drops and inspire one another to keep going when you run into difficulties. Your family and friends may not understand why you run a blog or how it feels to hit a slump, but your fellow bloggers can be there to offer support. Make sure that you reciprocate and keep the relationship evenly balanced.

As well as finding friends, you may be able to form a business relationship that could enable you to collaborate on projects such as additional websites, an eBook, or a consulting service. Before embarking on a collaboration with another blogger, take the time to get to know them as an individual and a potential business partner. Ask them whether they have collaborated with others and, if so, the degree to which their last project was successful.

If you are thinking of investing a significant amount of time or money on a joint project, it is a good idea to draw up a legally binding contract that specifies who will own the end product and how the proceeds will be split. Talking to a contract lawyer in the early stages could save you from later difficulties. You may also wish to consider working together on a smaller project first, in order to check that you are compatible as partners. Sometimes you may find that an individual is a great asset as a friend or peer, but that their personality or working style does not fit with your own.

Where to find other bloggers writing in your niche

Look at the blogs you already read

If you have chosen a blog topic about which you are passionate, you will already be reading blogs on the subject and probably have two or three favourites. Take the next step by following these bloggers on social media. Who do they follow and whose blogs do they read? Follow any links included in their posts. Create a bookmarks folder in your internet browser and fill it with links to the best blogs in your field.

Use search engines, to track down new bloggers

Another simple way of finding relevant blogs is to use search engines. Searching "blog" + "blog topic" will bring you many

74

helpful results, assuming that your interests are shared by others. If you cannot find any other relevant blogs, try using slightly different search terms. If this still doesn't work, it may be a sign that not many people are interested in your topic and that you will find it hard to attract a significant number of visitors to your blog.

Look at author biographies on news and current affairs sites

You have probably noticed that contributors writing for large lifestyle sites, such as the Huffington Post, often have brief biographies at the end of their articles. If you find an article that is relevant to your blog topic, look at the author's biography and check whether they have a blog. If so, read it and consider becoming a regular visitor. If their work is especially inspirational, leave them a few blog comments and follow them on social media. As will be addressed in greater depth later on in the course, writing and publishing articles on high traffic sites is a good way of attracting more visitors to your blog. It is also worth checking whether the authors of your favourite books maintain blogs, particularly if their work relates to your blog topic.

Look for blogging conferences targeted at those in your niche

Go to Google or any other search engine and type "blogging conference", followed by your country, or "online blogging conference", if you would prefer to network online or live in a small country. Along with large blogging conventions that target bloggers as a general group, there are conferences held for specific niches, such as beauty, fitness, home schooling and current affairs.

Once you begin searching for relevant events, you will discover listings for conferences, together with instructions on how to register. Most blog conferences have associated websites and social media pages that will tell you more about the event, including a list of guest speakers and any organisations that will be in attendance. Costs will vary, depending on the length and location of the conference. Don't forget to account for travel and accommodation expenses.

Blogging conferences often incorporate workshops designed to help bloggers excel at their craft and attract more traffic to their blogs.

Etiquette – how to reach out to another blogger in your niche

Blogging is a social activity and most bloggers will be receptive to brief friendly messages.

However, there are a few guidelines to remember when networking with others:

Do not send overly long or detailed messages

In the blogosphere, brevity is valued. Make initial contact with another blogger, by writing them a brief, positive comment on their blog, or by sending them a quick message on social media. Let them know that you appreciate their work, ideally by complimenting one of their recent posts. Follow them on social media, as appropriate (we will return to the ways in which you can best use social media whilst blogging later in the chapter) and provide them with brief, insightful comments, when they publish a particularly strong piece of content.

Make it easy for someone to find and review your work

If you use email to communicate with other bloggers, set up a signature that automatically adds your full name, blog address and any social media handles to the end of your messages. Do not assume that someone will remember your personal details the first, second, or even third time you repeat them.

Do not send a message asking for a favour

Just as it is generally unacceptable to ask a stranger on the street for a favour, it is inappropriate to make your first contact with another blogger a request for help.
Try to build a relationship with them first or help them out in some small way – perhaps by mentioning one of their articles on your blog and then tweeting them the link to your post. Most bloggers will not take kindly to requests from someone they have never heard of before. If they are especially popular or famous in your niche, they are likely to be too busy to work with a stranger who has not even offered them a favour in return.

If you do not get a response, do not take it personally

Most people now have multiple demands on their time and as a result, struggle to respond to every email or message they receive. If you get in touch with a blogger and do not get a reply, do not assume that you have done anything wrong. In all likelihood, they are simply too busy and will respond if and when they have the time. It is generally acceptable to send one or at most two "follow-up" or reminder messages, spaced at least two weeks apart.

Always keep your tone upbeat and friendly

Whether you are leaving a comment on someone's blog or sending them an email asking whether they would like to write a guest post for your site, always be pleasant and positive. If you gain a reputation for being difficult or unfriendly, your blog's popularity will suffer and others will be less willing to work with you.
Moreover, making negative comments will encourage others to conclude that you are a generally critical or even jealous individual, who is best avoided. The old saying "If you can't say anything nice, say nothing" applies, when you network with other bloggers.

Remember that content you send via the internet will be around forever

Following on from the previous point, remember that the recipients of your emails, blog comments and social media posts will be able to keep copies of whatever you send or publish. Think very carefully, before commenting on sensitive topics or making controversial statements, particularly if you do not know the recipient well. It is hard to convey tone via text and therefore, it is easier to cause offence online than it is in person.

If you want to re-post any content, ask permission first

Linking to someone else's blog post, together with a positive comment, is a good strategy for networking, as it shows an appreciation for someone else's work. However, if you wish to post more than a brief excerpt or quote from someone else's blog, send them a message asking permission first. Most bloggers work hard to put together original content and do not respond well to their posts being reused without prior consultation. They may even have grounds to take legal action against you for copyright infringement, even if you cite your source and link to the original version.

Always ask a blogger before re-purposing their content.

Tell them why you wish to use it on your own blog and reassure them that you will give them credit, as appropriate. Keep a copy of any messages in which they grant you permission to use their material. If they decline to grant you permission, do not press them for an explanation. It is their right to retain control over their intellectual property.

14. Using social media to amplify and increase reach of your blog

It is not realistic to set up a blog, publish some content and then hope that readers will stumble across it whilst searching for relevant topics via Google or another search engine. As you publish more content, your blog pages will be indexed by the major search engines, meaning that when someone types in relevant search terms, your page (amongst many others) will be returned in the results list.

Google do not release comprehensive information on the algorithms used to rank webpages, in order to minimise the chance that people will attempt to "game" the system. Even if you regularly update your blog with plenty of high quality content, it may take weeks or even months before it attracts visitors arriving via search engine results. You will need to use other means of attracting readers and a popular strategy to generate blog traffic is to utilise social media. By posting attractive content that signposts other members of a social network to your blog and by networking with others who share your interests, you can start to build your blog's reputation, before it ranks highly in search engine results.

The most popular social media platforms for bloggers

The following is an overview of the social media websites you should consider using to promote your blog, connect with potential readers and network with other bloggers:

<u>Twitter (twitter.com)</u>

When you sign up to Twitter, you create a page containing a brief biography and a list of short updates (280 characters or less) known as "Tweets". Some people refer to Twitter as a microblogging platform, as a user's tweets can be likened to very short blog posts. Twitter currently has over 300 million users all around the world, giving you access to numerous target markets.

One of Twitter's best-known features is its hashtag system. When you write a tweet, you can include hashtags that relate to its content. When other users search for a particular hashtag using the site's search function, any tweets you write making use of that hashtag will appear in the search results. This allows Twitter users to locate content that is of particular interest to them.

As a blogger, you can make good use of this function to draw other peoples' attention to your content.

Twitter will also provide you with recommendations regarding who you should consider following, based on your interests. This is a great way to meet other bloggers. When you follow someone new, look in their profile box and follow any links to blogs or other websites listed. From the moment you follow them, their activity will appear on your Twitter feed. You can send and receive public tweets that will show up on your feed, or if you and another person are following one another, you can communicate via private messages.

When responding to someone else's tweets, you can use "@[theirusername]", to ensure that their attention is drawn to your message.

You can quickly and easily indicate your appreciation of someone else's content and pass on it on to your followers (a practice known as "retweeting"), which can improve your reputation and encourage others to share your content in return.

Facebook

Facebook is the best known of the social networks. As of the first quarter of 2018, Facebook had 2.19 billion monthly active users. In the third quarter of 2012, the number of active Facebook users had surpassed one billion, making it the first social network ever to do so.
When you join Facebook, you will be able to set up a page to promote your blog. You can post updates that keep your "fans" (other users who have chosen to "Like" your page) notified of your recent activity, such as new blog posts. You can search for other people and organisations with similar interests and make new connections. If you want to set up a page for your blog or business, it is important to note that you will also need to create a personal account if you do not have one already. Although you can use Facebook to highlight other peoples' content, it is generally less acceptable to do so than it is on Twitter. Those who have chosen to follow your page will be hoping to see content that you have written, so focus on your own material at least 80% of the time.

LinkedIn (linkedin.com)

LinkedIn is a good option, if your blog targets or will appeal to a more commercially minded audience. For example, if you write about leadership, productivity, time management or career related subjects, then consider setting up a LinkedIn profile for yourself and your brand. To create a professional first impression, upload a banner relevant to your blog that fits with your site's overall design and colour scheme. You can have these made for just a few pounds, via a freelancing platform such as Fiverr (fiverr.com) or Upwork (upwork.com). Be sure to keep both your personal and blog related profiles active.

You can use LinkedIn to connect with people you have met or worked with in a professional capacity or educational setting. Look up your old college acquaintances, your colleagues past and present and any bloggers or business owners you have been in contact with since setting up your website. Whenever you make friends with a fellow blogger, look them up and invite them to connect with you.

An extremely useful means of finding other bloggers and business owners within your niche is via LinkedIn Groups. As recorded in March 2018 there were 2.1 million groups on the site; the majority of users sign up to (or are invited to join) at least one of them. This facility offers excellent networking opportunities and the chance to make your name more widely known. When you log in to your LinkedIn profile, you can identify groups to join by clicking on the "Interests" tab followed by "Groups". You can search for groups or use the suggestions presented to you by the site's algorithms. If you can't find a group that fits with your interests, create your own.

Another useful networking strategy to employ on LinkedIn is to follow "Influencers" – those who have many contacts and are considered key players in their industries – and engage with them and their communities. You can do this by paying close attention to their updates and posting thoughtful questions in response to their content.

Instagram

Instagram is an image based social media platform. Users post photos and other images with captions which can then be shared by others. It is especially popular with bloggers whose content lends itself to visual communication. For example, bloggers writing about fashion and beauty often post photos of new outfits or makeup products. Artists, photographers and designers can also make good use of Instagram to promote their products. When undertaking a large project, producers can engage with their audience by posting "teaser" photographs showing various stages.

Instagram can also be an effective means of providing your audience with a personal insight into your everyday life. It takes only seconds to photograph a place or object that illustrates a project, an idea, or your workspace. This can help create a rapport between you and your readers. Instagram is a fast moving platform and to maintain engagement with your audience, it is best to post several times per day.

Rather than posting text excerpts from blog posts, Instagram images are best used as advertisements for and gateways to blog posts. Instagram also allows its users to employ hashtags, in order to mark content and find other posts and users of interest.

Pinterest

Pinterest encourages users to create collections of content that centre around one or more themes. When you sign up for an account, you will be asked to create your first "Board", which is a collection of image based pieces of content around a theme of your choice. You can browse other peoples' content, follow those with interests related to your blog and then save (or "pin") posts that you would like in your own collections.

Bloggers can use Pinterest to engage with potential readers and to network with others who may be interested in their content.

You could compile a new board whenever you release a new blog post, although this may not be an efficient use of your time until you have a significant number of followers. An alternative approach that may be more time effective is to create boards based around the major themes or common threads that run through your blog posts. To continue with the wedding blog example above, you might decide to create boards around the themes of vintage wedding décor, contemporary wedding décor, budget décor ideas and so on.

How to use social media posts, statuses and updates to drive visitors to your blog
Once you have set up your accounts on social media, you can start producing posts that drive visitors to your blog.

Follow these guidelines to entice viewers to go beyond simply reading your posts and actively choose to click through to your full length articles:

Post intriguing titles, together with a link to your full content

Never publish a post with a boring title. Make your headlines as concise and interesting as possible. The most effective titles promise to entertain the reader, to let them in on an important piece of information, to tell them a secret, or give them the steps required to solve a problem.

Use images in conjunction with engaging quotes, to encourage readers to view the full article

It takes significantly less time for a viewer to process an image than a paragraph or even a short sentence. Use an attention grabbing photo, illustration, graph, or cartoon, along with a meaningful caption to communicate your message in just a couple of seconds.

If you are writing about content that has been covered by many other people, do your best to make it seem fresh and exciting

If possible, create blog posts that invite viewers to consider an issue or problem from a new perspective. However, if you are writing about a topic that has already been covered by numerous other bloggers in your niche, use your creativity to stimulate your readers' curiosity. For example, if you were to publish a blog post about the basic science of calorie counting – as many others before you have done – you could promote your content by describing it as "the timeless secret to lasting weight loss you need to know!"

Make it easy for blog readers to share your content

Your readers are your allies in spreading links to your blog and thereby raising your public profile.

Make sure that your blog readers always have the option of posting a link to your content on their social media network of choice. This is easy to do with tools and plugins that come with most blogging platforms and services.

There is some debate in the blogosphere as to whether you should ask your readers to share their favourite articles via social media. On one hand, some argue that when readers come across an outstanding piece of content, they are likely to share it with little prompting. Moreover, readers may be annoyed if you frequently implore them to share links.

At the same time, a simple request such as "If you liked this, please pass it on!" written next to social media buttons at the end of an article can encourage readers who would not have otherwise bothered.

Try both approaches on your blog to see which works best, as results may vary according to your audience's characteristics and the style in which your blog is written.

How To Make Effective Use Of Images And Other Visual Media

Why you should not rely on text alone

Whilst there will always be people who prefer to obtain information via the written word, images and videos add an extra dimension to your blog content.

Your blog readers now have more demands on their time than ever before – and an increasing number of options, when it comes to deciding how they will spend their time online. Adding visual media can make your readers feel more interested in your content, meaning that they are more likely to return to your site at a later date. Moreover, incorporating images can also help you to enjoy the process of blogging, as it can be an effective means of creative expression.

The best times to make use of visual media on your blog

Certain types of blog post lend themselves especially well to images and videos.
Here are some instances in which you may wish to consider adding another media element:

When you are writing a personal post

A personal photo or portrait allows your audience to connect with you on an immediate level and gain a sense of your personality, surroundings and daily routine. If you want to appeal to your audience's emotions, a video in which you and others speak directly to the
camera can be highly effective.

When you are reporting on an event or experience

Good writing can transport the reader to a new place and convey how it felt to experience something special, but images are a valuable supplement to even the most well-chosen of words. For example, if you have recently attended a major conference that will be of interest to your readers, posting a few photos of the crowds and most popular trade stands will give them a greater sense of what it was like to be in attendance, rather than a few paragraphs of written description.

When you wish to review a product or service

If you are writing about a product for the purposes of review or promotion, your readers will appreciate an image showing what it is you are describing. This will encourage them to take your review more seriously and help them to envisage how the product looks and performs. You could take a photograph of the image in its original packaging, followed by a video showing how it performs during use. If you write a positive review, send the company an email or social media message and let them know. If they like your post, they may spread a link to your blog via their own blog or social media channels. This can be an effective means of generating extra traffic to your site.

When you want to break a difficult concept down into simple ideas

Infographics are a popular way for bloggers to convey ideas using a combination of text, shapes, colour and graphics. They are an effective way of communicating various steps that make up a procedure or presenting a series of statistics that provide the reader with an overview of the important facts on a particular topic. You can make your own infographics using software that you may already have, such as Microsoft Word or PowerPoint. There are also online services that help you create infographics to use, at little or zero cost.

When you want to demonstrate how your audience can best carry out a project or learn a new skill

Tutorials are often best presented as a series of images, or in video form.

The public domain

Some material is available for anyone to use in whatever way they wish, with no restrictions whatsoever and no obligation to credit the original creator.

Such material is said to be "in the public domain". The rules around the public domain vary between countries, but in general a piece of content passes into the public domain 70 years following the death of its creator. This rule applies to music, text, film and visual media. However, a creator can also decide to release their work into the public domain whenever they choose. Furthermore, much of the content produced by the UK and US governments is also in the public domain from the time it is created.

When you use an image that is in the public domain, you are free to publish it, change it and use it as the basis for your own works, without fear of legal action. The Public Domain Review (publicdomainreview.org) is a good resource for learning more about the concept of the public domain and for finding images you can use with no restrictions. Pixabay (pixabay.com) is a library of public domain images – mostly of a contemporary nature – which is updated frequently.

Making your own images and videos

There are several advantages to creating your own visual media, rather than using those created by someone else:

It could save you money

If you need to find an image depicting an unusual object or subject matter, the number of free images available for you to use may be limited and you may have to pay money to use material from a stock photo website. Taking your own photographs can save you this expense. With some effort and imagination, you will probably be able to capture a shot that will perfectly illustrate the points made within your blog post. **It will ensure that you will avoid any legal problems later on**

When you personally produce a piece of media for your own use, you know for certain that you own the copyright and are therefore free to do with it exactly as you wish.

You will not have to worry whether you have properly understood any terms and conditions associated with the image, as it is your intellectual property.

It gives you the chance to express yourself

Taking your own photographs and scripting your own videos forces you to use your creativity and communicate your message in a unique way. It can be a rewarding process that allows you to develop potentially transferable skills. If you want to further your skillset, you could invest in some image editing software such as Photoshop. In producing material for your website, you could take the first steps towards a new career.

It may provide you with a product to sell later on

If you are able to take high quality photographs, you may be able to sell them to stock image sites later on. You can also use images to sell merchandise via platforms such as CafePress (cafepress.com) and Zazzle (zazzle.com). These sites allow you to upload your photographs, graphics and illustrations to be printed onto T-shirts, mugs and other products that are printed and sold on demand. If you want to open an online shop with products unique to your blog, creating images can be the first step to marketing your own merchandise.

It will lend your blog a degree of individuality

When you use images and videos that you have created, your blog will stand out from others. Everyone has their own style and if you consistently produce your own media, your audience will come to recognise and appreciate your unique brand.

Optimising your visual content

The best way of attracting traffic from search engines is to produce a blog made up of high quality, relevant, long form written content.

However, there are also steps you can take when using images and videos to help your website appear early on in the list of search engine results. When you insert an image into a blog post using your blogging software or platform of choice, you will be given the opportunity to describe the image using text based descriptions known as "tags". When a search engine trawls the internet looking for content relevant to a user's search, it will not only register the text in your written posts, but also the tags associated with any images you have chosen to use.

When optimising the images on your blog, your two primary considerations ought to be Alt tags and Title tags. The way in which you will edit these tags will depend on the blogging platform you are using, but the following is an overview of their purpose and a few tips on how to improve your images' performance:

Use keywords in your file names

When you take a photograph and upload it to your site, make sure that the image has a descriptive, relevant file name, before you include it in your post. For example, if you take a photograph your camera may automatically label the image as "image_001.jpg", which will not allow a search engine to determine the content of the file. Instead, use a filename that accurately portrays whatever you have captured within the image.

Make good use of the alt tags

If you have ever tried to load a webpage only to realise that an image has not displayed properly, you will know that within every image on the internet is a text based description of the content. If an image cannot be displayed, the alt tag is the text that will appear in its place. You can sometimes see the alt tag, when you hover the mouse over a fully loaded image. It is best to use honest, straightforward descriptions in your alt tags. It may be tempting to fill the tag with keywords in the hope that your site will be ranked higher in search engine results, but this is counterproductive as Google and other search engines make use of sophisticated algorithms that can detect likely instances of someone trying to "game the system".

Show multiple angles or views of the same product if you are writing a review

If you have a good reason to include several shots of the same product in a blog post, then take the opportunity to do so.

This allows you to include multiple alt tags on one page, all containing keywords that can help draw visitors to your site via search engine results.

General guidelines for using images effectively

Ensure that your images are of an appropriate size

Excessively large images can confuse your readers, as they will wonder why you have felt the need to include an image that takes up so much space on the page. At the same time, small images can frustrate readers who will not appreciate having to squint at the screen or zoom in to fathom the subject matter. Look at other blogs in your niche and take note of how they use images. How large are their photos and illustrations and where do they position them on the page?

Do not use too many images

Only use relevant images that add value to your post. Including images for the sake of it will not enhance your readers' experience and in fact, may discourage them from returning to your blog. It is better to choose just one or two suitable illustrations, than to incorporate as many as possible. Furthermore, an excess of images can cause delays in page loading times, which will irritate your visitors.

Take or find only high quality images

If you are taking your own photos, take the time to learn how to shoot clear images in which the subject matter can be clearly seen. If you are using images from the internet, make sure that they convey the right tone – quality and professionalism – and look aesthetically pleasing, before publishing them as part of a blog post. Using blurry, badly edited, or inappropriate images will communicate to your audience that you have not devoted much time or effort to your blog, which may in turn lead them to question why they should bother reading it.

Check that your images look good on both desktop and mobile versions of your site

Many of your visitors will be viewing your blog on mobile devices rather than traditional desktop monitors. It is therefore essential that your images load easily on both kinds of device. Most blogging platforms are now automatically optimised for mobile viewing, but you should still be sure to preview your posts on large and small screens before publishing.

Place your image immediately to one side of the first paragraph of your article

An image reduces the amount of text confronting the reader, when they take their first glance at an article. When you use an inline image, the lines of text immediately to the left or right will appear shorter, making it easier for the viewer to get drawn in.
This provides you with an opportunity to hook the reader in and encourage them to read an article in its entirety.

Include images of people and animals rather than, or in addition to, objects

As social creatures, humans tend to enjoy looking at other people. We also find animals (especially furry mammals and domestic pets) aesthetically appealing. Make these the focus of your blog images, where possible. If you need to feature images of objects, try to find some way of incorporating a human or animal presence if possible.

Avoid clichéd stock photos

Once you have spent a few minutes looking at the material available on major stock photo websites – whether free or paid – you will start to notice that certain themes and visual clichés appear on a frequent basis. As a general rule, you should not use any image that has a "familiar" feel to it, or that your readers might recognise as a cliché.
Another common mistake is to use stock photographs of models, who are pulling unnatural facial expressions. Unless you are writing an article about unnatural expressions, do not use this kind of material on your blog. It is distracting and may give the impression that you do not know how to identify normal human faces. Remember – only use an image if it is relevant to the point you are making in a blog post and fits with your site's message as a whole.

Make use of free online software to improve the appearance of images on your blog

There are many websites that offer you tools to develop and refine images, whether you created them yourself or are using someone else's work with permission.

15. How to use your blog to attract customer to your business

An increasing number of businesses are making the most of the internet, in order to promote their products and services.

For traditional offline businesses such as shops and restaurants, a blog is a great way of establishing credibility, building a rapport with customers and giving you an edge over your competition. Once you have set up a business blog, it should only take a couple of hours per week to maintain, if you have drawn up a posting schedule and a plan detailing what points will be addressed in each post.

The main benefits for your business are as follows:

It will make your business easier to find

If your blog contains high quality content about your business and related topics, there is a greater chance that it will appear high up in lists of search engine results when someone types in terms such as "[your industry/product type]" + "[location]". This is a crucial first step in attracting visitors to your site, who may then become customers. In addition, you can post excerpts of your posts to your business's social media platforms. When presented in an attractive way, these links will encourage readers to visit your website. From there, you can use sales copy, product descriptions and other content, to encourage visitors to spend money with you.

It will improve the relationship you have with your customers and encourage new customers to make their first purchase

A well designed website with useful content will go a long way in cementing a positive relationship and improving your reputation. It signals to your customers that you take their experience and opinions seriously, and that you are willing to spend time and effort creating
a good impression with your target market.

It will help you gain credibility within your industry

When you post helpful, relevant and engaging content to your blog, others will begin to perceive you as a trusted source and as an authority within your niche.
If you run a business specialising in care solutions for elderly patients, a well-researched blog post on how to choose the most appropriate care home may be well received by your audience.

Types of posts you can use to engage with your target audience

Once you have drawn up a posting schedule, ensure that the person responsible for your business communications and marketing coordinates the production and publication of blog content.

You should be as consistent as possible. When an existing or potential customer arrives at your website, they should get the impression that you have put thought into devising a long-term blogging and social media strategy. This creates a more balanced website and a more professional image.

It is much better to post once a week for two years, than to publish a flurry of posts over a couple of months before suffering from blog burnout.

Consider including the following kinds of post on your business blog:

Tutorial posts

If you sell products that may be difficult for your customers to use, why not create a video tutorial showing them how to get the most from their purchase?
Tutorial posts show your audience that you not only want to sell them products and services, but also that you care about the success of their projects. If you can produce a video showing real customers using your products, this will also serve the purpose of acting as a positive testimonial.

Posts that introduce members of a team

People like to do business with those that inspire within them feelings of trust. One of the best ways of building this sense of security is to use your blog as a platform by which your customers can get to know the people behind the business. Include an "About Us" page on your website, listing the core members of staff, together with a clear headshot of each person and a brief description of their role within the company. You could also run a series of blog posts in which employees take it in turns to write about a specific topic, promote a product or service they personally endorse, or to talk about their experience of working for the company.

Posts that spell out the company's purpose or mission

Make sure that your customers and prospective customers understand not only who you are as an organisation, but what you are trying to do. Why did the founder start the business in the first place? Were they driven by a particular personal need, or perhaps they saw a gap in the market that they knew how to fill? What principles, aims and values drive the development of the business in its current form? These questions can provide you with a solid foundation for a blog post.

Posts that build excitement around an upcoming product or service

If you have started to stock, develop or offer a product or service you think will be popular with your target market, use your blog as a means of promoting it. Write a post in which you introduce the product or service, why it is of interest to your target market and when it will be available to buy.

If you are considering whether to stock a particular product line, you could create a post in which you solicit your readers' opinions. This could be as simple as creating a poll or quiz within a blog post and asking readers to select which option most appeals to them. You could ask them to select their favourite product from a list, or ask them to tell you what problems or projects they have been tackling recently in their hobby or line of work, as appropriate.

Posts that highlight a current or upcoming job opportunity

If your business is small and close-knit, posts describing job vacancies can be a positive way of providing potential candidates with useful background information to read, prior to submitting an application. In addition, it can be an effective means of giving your customers an insight into your recruitment process and the qualities you value in an employee.

Posts that provide the reader with a background on a particular topic

Think about the most pressing concerns amongst members of your target audience. For example, if you run a business that sells maternity clothes, it is likely that your customers will be concerned with issues such as dressing well for formal occasions whilst pregnant, how to maintain a positive body image before and after birth and what materials are most comfortable to wear for women approaching their due date. You could ask suitably qualified professionals to take part in an interview for your blog, using either a set of questions you have devised or queries from your blog readers. Use images as appropriate, to illustrate your points.

Using a blog to show your organisation's personality

A good business blog strikes the right balance between personality and professionalism.

Although you should always remember that you are writing for business rather than social purposes, people prefer to read engaging, informal text, as opposed to dry or formal content. With this in mind, make your posts as readable as possible. Write as though you were addressing one of your everyday customers. Avoid excessive use of jargon and if you must introduce a technical term, then be sure to include a short definition. Improve an article's readability, by breaking it down into brief paragraphs and keeping sentences succinct.

It is acceptable to use an informal tone and use personal pronouns if it fits with your business image, but avoid vulgar language and crude humour.
You can also build credibility by making reference to relevant facts and figures. If you are writing an article promoting a particular product, you could use statistics that highlight a consumer need or trigger an emotive response.

How to make use of social media, to attract new customers

With a significant proportion of the population using social media on a regular basis, most businesses benefit from developing a strong social media presence.
Although it can take some time to learn the basics, social media has two main advantages – you can reach millions of people and you can spread your message at no cost whatsoever.
Your first step is to identify which platform is best suited to the nature of your business and to your target audience.

If your business is small, then you may not have the resources to maintain multiple social media platforms and so will need to choose how to spread the time that is available to you. Once you have chosen your platform, you will need to create a professional looking profile page. You can create attractive backgrounds and banners yourself, or hire a freelance professional to do it for you.

Your blog and social media profiles should be closely linked from the beginning. Don't forget to make it easy for your followers to click through to your blog.

When you post a new piece of content to your blog, be sure to notify your social media followers. Do not post the full article – instead, think of your social media updates as "bait" that will hopefully lure your followers to your blog and engage their interest.

16. Keeping backups of your content

Your blog is at risk of complete erasure should it come under attack.

This is why it is vital that you keep backup copies of your content. If you are using an all in one platform such as Blogger, Tumblr or Wix, you should familiarise yourself with their backup functions as soon as you set up a blog. Usually, these platforms have simple one-click options that allow you to save a copy of your site to your computer. In the event of a security breach, you can use this backup (following advice from the provider as necessary) to restore your blog.

If you are using a self-hosted WordPress site, you should use a plugin that automatically creates and stores a copy of your blog.

BackupBuddy costs around £60 per year, whereas UpdraftPlus is available in both free and premium versions, the latter costing from £50 per year. These plugins come with helpful customer support, the ability to create backups on a schedule of your choosing (e.g. daily, weekly, or monthly) and the option to send a copy of your website files to an email or online storage facility, such as Dropbox (dropbox.com).

www.ingramcontent.com/pod-product-compliance
Lightning Source LLC
Chambersburg PA
CBHW070049210526
45170CB00012B/623